PEEK-A-BOO, I SEE YOU

SPIRITUAL WARFARE AGAINST THINGS THAT GO BUMP IN THE NIGHT

VANESSA M. WHITE

WESTBOW
PRESS®
A DIVISION OF THOMAS NELSON
& ZONDERVAN

WestBow Press books may be ordered through booksellers or by contacting:

WestBow Press
A Division of Thomas Nelson & Zondervan
1663 Liberty Drive
Bloomington, IN 47403
www.westbowpress.com
844-714-3454

Interior Graphics/Art Credit: Xander Austin

ISBN: 979-8-3850-1201-5 (sc)
ISBN: 979-8-3850-1200-8 (e)

Print information available on the last page.

WestBow Press rev. date: 12/14/2023

DEDICATION

This book is dedicated to the Holy Father and His son, Jesus Christ.

CONTENTS

ACKNOWLEDGMENTS

I acknowledge the following people who were there for me on my book-writing journey.

To my pastor, Reverend Tommy Hall, who preaches the Word of God in season and out, thank you for being a living example of Christ.

To Sheila Morris, who is a great listener and has been the best sounding board for my writing, "You go, girl!"

To my stepsister, Petreane Middleton, whose voice I still hear in my ears saying, "Vanesa, when are you going to write your book?" You are awesome, Sis.

To Apostle Mary Rogers-Iles, who constantly asked me, "What did God say about it?" and "Did you check with God first?" I hate to admit it, but you were so right.

To all the foster parents who give their time, love, and

resources to help children who are not their own, Bravo! Foster parents, Bravo!

To Reverend Barbara C. White, Pastor, and retired schoolteacher, thank you for yielding that stick of correction of God's word in my life and my writing. May the Lord bless you ever so much.

PREFACE

During my lifetime, I have been around children. I have worked for and with them and have even been a child myself. I have seen broken hearts and wounded spirits of children who have been mentally, emotionally, and physically traumatized from the environment they lived in. I have witnessed children joyously laughing as well as crying bitter tears. I have seen children so deeply depressed that they try to commit suicide. Some have even succeeded at killing themselves. This saddens me to the point where I wanted to do something about it. I want to become an advocate and fight for the children. My heart goes out to children of every race, creed, or color in this world. They are God's little people whom he loves dearly. Being sent to this earth to grow and develop in the ways of God, makes them very special. It has been my mission in life to protect children. I will do so until my time to leave the battlefield is over. Therefore, I wrote this book.

INTRODUCTION

This book is not for the faint of heart. Nor is it for those who are afraid of dark spiritual warfare. God's Holy Spirit empowers us to see through this fallen world's mist, muck, and mess. You must remember, children of God, that this world is not your home. Reading this book will help you overcome the forces of evil that are set out to destroy you and your children. This book is an informational and educational guide to help protect you and your family. I have experience working in jails and prisons for 24 and a half years. I have seen devastating things there. That is how I can write about experiences in this book. I am also like a cuckoo clock, trying to wake up parents and guardians, letting them know that they can prevail against all forces of evil that want to annihilate their kids. This book will help you act and walk your family toward the kingdom of God.

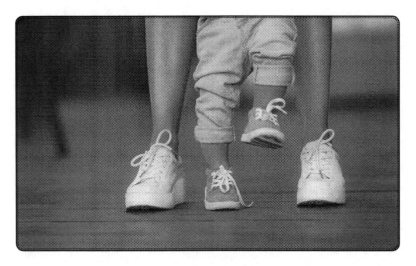

CHAPTER 1

Man Out of Mankind

The Bible says that in the beginning, God created the heavens and the earth. Genesis 2:1-2 tells the account of God finishing his work of creation and resting. When he made Adam and Eve, he put the mechanism in place for them to be fruitful, multiply and fill the earth with people. The population of people who are born into the world becomes what is called mankind. God gave us the power to reproduce. God provides us with a body, mind, and spirit at conception. Therefore, we come into this world fully capable. We all know that adults start as little children. It is these little children we must protect. Yes, children are a gift from God. Our Heavenly Father is the one who created the family. He sent the Holy Spirit to put the baby Jesus in Mary's womb.

Jesus grew up and was an example of how we should live on this earth as children of God (John 3:1-2). From the book of Genesis to Revelation, God talks about the importance of children in his family. According to scripture, the priorities in the family should be God, spouse, children, grandparents, relatives, and spiritual family such as brothers and sisters in Christ. The rest of the world would be considered the family of mankind. We must protect these people so that they can become productive members of society.

CHAPTER 2

Transformation (From natural to spiritual)

G od is a Spirit, and we worship him in spirit and truth (John 4:24). Some Christians forget that we are body, mind, and spirit. God created us in his image and likeness, which is Spirit. God formed us from the dust of the ground and then blew breath of life in us, and we became living souls. It was God who put it all together. When we get saved and filled with the Holy Spirit, we are transformed from flesh to Spirit. Our minds are illuminated, allowing us to see, walk, talk, and feel in the spiritual realm.

All children have a body, mind, soul, and spirit too. As he fights you, Satan attacks the children on all levels. Because they are not saved, filled with the Holy Spirit, and their minds are not transformed, they are heavily bombarded by evil. They are helpless and do not know spiritual warfare yet. The positive side is that parents or guardians have spiritual authority over their children until they reach the age of accountability (Romans 13:1-2). When the Lord loaned us his children, he gave us control over them. Romans 13:1-2 lets us know that all authority comes from God, and everyone must submit to it.

God gave the Holy Spirit, who does the work of transforming the mind. He changes thoughts from conforming to the patters of this world to the righteousness of the word of God. He transforms believers into Godly living and away from selfish, fleshly, carnal living. He also changes believers from walking in the darkness to the light of Christ (Ephesians 5:8; John 8:12; John 1:4). When you walk in the light of God's love, you won't stumble and fall. You won't get trapped in Satan's spiritual spider webs used to entangle us. But, when you don't take authority over your children's lives, you leave the door open for evil beings to attack them. Then you can surely expect punishment to come for your neglect and rebellion (1 Samuel 15:23). We Christians claim that we are kings and priests over our homes. But rebellion to God's word and authority knocks us off the throne. So, let's be spiritual watchdogs and guard ourselves and our families.

CHAPTER 3

Spiritual Blindness

When you have been transformed from flesh to spirit, your spiritual eyes, ears, and other senses are activated. Consequently, if you have eyes to see, then let them see. If you have ears to hear, then listen. John 3:19-21 tells us that light came into the world, but people loved darkness more than light. At one time we were spiritually dead because of sins against God. But the Father had mercy and gave us a new life in Christ (Ephesians 2:4-5). Through the shed blood of Jesus, we became spiritually alive and can see into the spiritual realm. Of course, the devil, our adversary, did not like that one bit. He counteracted by blinding the eyes of those who do not believe in Christ (1 Corinthians 4:4-6). The question is, if you are spiritually blind, how can you fight something that you cannot see? How will you fight against things that go bump in the night when you can't see them hiding under your child's bed or in his closet? Little Johnny can see it. Why can't you?

In the natural world, a blind man cannot join the army and go to war. The same goes for the spiritual world. Can a parent or guardian protect his child if he cannot see and still plays around in darkness with evil? When the demons come to take your child, how will you stop them? The 1980s singer-songwriter Ray Parker Jr. wrote the song *Ghost Busters*. It was used as the theme song for the Hollywood movie of the same name. The song repeated the phrase, "Who you gonna call? Ghostbusters!" several times. I'm only asking you who you will call to save your child, once. I sincerely hope it's not the ghostbusters. Jesus is the light of the world. In him is no darkness (John 1:4-5). When we follow Jesus, we see evil hiding to destroy our children. We have the power to fight back. It is a fact that the darkness of evil can never overcome the light of Christ. In the Bible, Jesus constantly identified demons and cast them off people. He knew them in Heaven before he came to the earth. They remembered him too and were afraid of him (John 1:1-5; Luke 4:41 NLT).

Those who refuse the light of Christ remain in spiritual darkness and sin unless they come to Jesus and get born again. John 3:20 tells us that everyone who does evil hates the light. They don't want their sinful deeds exposed by the light (this includes people and evil spirits). However, we, as believers, walk in the light. We love the light that Christ put inside of us because it shines in the dark like a high-beam flashlight. Therefore, we can expose those things done in the darkness (Ephesians 5:8-14). We can tell those unholy beings, Peek-a-Boo, I see you. We can say to them that God has opened my eyes, and I know what you are doing. I have the power and authority to cast you out. The war is on, and I will protect my children from you and your cohorts.

CHAPTER 4

Spiritual Warfare

God's army is like man's army —you must sign up, be trained, and become prepared for war; then, you fight your country's battles. In God's army, you must be saved, born again, and faithfully follow God's word to fight spiritual battles. Spiritual warfare is unavoidable for Christians. The action begins as soon as believers accept Jesus Christ as their Lord and Savior.

Christ died to save us from sin and the power of darkness. He died to restore us to righteousness with his Father, God. His shed blood washed away our sins and gave us the right to the Tree of Life; believers must be saved to receive this right (Genesis 2:9; Revelation 22:2, 14, 19). The process of salvation begins with believers' repenting of sins and believing in their hearts that God raised them from the dead. From these actions, believers sign up for spiritual warfare in God's army. Welcome aboard!

The following Stage is the rebirth or walking in new life. An example is Nicodemus, one of the few Pharisees or high-ranking religious leaders who believed in Christ. Being a high official did not stop the Lord Jesus from letting Nicodemus know that he had to be born again (John 3:1-7).

Nicodemus had to be regenerated by the Holy Spirit to function in the spiritual realm. Repentance and spiritual rebirth are required to enter the Kingdom of God. No flesh is allowed in Heaven.

Why do some believers and non-believers think they can fight in a spiritual arena with fleshly weapons? For example, they run to psychics, witch doctors, or shamans to guide them into the spirit realm. They also use psychotropic medications and psychedelic drugs to enter the spirit realm. These people don't understand that these behaviors open the gates to demonic possession of their and their children's souls. They don't understand the magnitude.

Zachariah 4:6 (KJV) tells us, "Not by might nor by power but by my spirit says the Lord." Spiritual warfare is real. This war that we are engaged in started in Heaven and is continued on Earth (Revelation 12:7-17). Satan (the adversary) was one of God's archangels. His name, Lucifer means the light bringer. God created him full of wisdom and beauty. His beauty and brilliance brought light to all those around him. Because of his beauty, Lucifer lifted himself in pride and rebellion and wanted to be God. He wanted other beings to worship him. Jesus, on the other hand, showed his humility while teaching his disciples to pray by acknowledging that God is sovereign. We are to worship God only (Exodus 20:1-3).

Satan was confused. He and the corrupted angels tried to usurp God's throne. He is an angel created to serve God. He was not made to be God. He was out of order and believed himself to be better than the Almighty God. He thought himself right and God wrong. However, the LORD God showed him who was right and wrong. God put Lucifer's light out and expelled him from Heaven (Isaiah 14:12).

God created light and has the right to do whatever he wanted to do with it. All that sin, rebellion, and lawlessness went out of Heaven to the dark side with Lucifer, now called Satan (Revelation 12:9-10; Luke 10:18 ESV). No longer walking in the light, he does his sneaky, evil deeds in the dark while still pretending to be an angel of the morning (2 Corinthians 11:14). In the Garden of Eden, he deceived Adam and Eve. Following him, their acts of rebellion opened the door for all kinds of evil to come into this world. Their sin propelled humanity into darkness with the devil and his demons. Adam and Eve both lost their spiritual eyesight. They became spiritually blind and afraid of the light. God is light, and they became fearful of him and hid from him (Genesis 3:8-10).

Not only is God light, but he is love. Love dwells in the light (Genesis 1:3-4). We can know love in our hearts and follow God's truths (2 Corinthians 4:6). Once again, since Satan has been put in the dark, he disguises himself as an angel of light to deceive humanity.

He tries to hoodwink weak Christians who don't read or study their Bible much and have little or no time for God. He goes after those with no personal or intimate relationship with the Father, Son, or Holy Spirit. He wants to drag those people into darkness and damnation with him and the fallen angels. But thank God for Jesus. The light shines in the darkness, and darkness cannot understand it (John 1:3-5). Jesus shines the light so mankind can see how to return to the Father. What the first man, Adam, lost, the second Adam, Jesus Christ, bought back by shedding his blood on Calvary's cross.

Satan wants to rule over us in darkness, yet Jesus' arms are still stretched to us daily. Satan hates God and cannot get back at him, so he goes after the weakest vessels, us, the children of God. He also goes after the next generation, which is our offspring. That is why we must stand in the gap and be a covering for the children. In Biblical times, cities were surrounded by walls protecting people from their enemies. If the wall was breached, the city could be demolished. Often it was burned or destroyed. Brave people would risk their lives by standing in the space of the broken wall to defend their city. Christians stand in the gap for our children, families, and others. We expose ourselves to Satan's fiery darts to protect the vulnerable ones. Moses stood in the gap for the children of Israel. Abraham stood in the gap for his nephew, Lot. The Lord Jesus stood in the gap for us. Our sins caused the wall to be left wide open for God's wrath to come down and judgment to enter and destroy us. The LORD Jesus stood in the gap, thus averting Divine punishment that was rightfully ours. Satan is ever vigilant in trying to put holes in the wall. He puts up smoke screens and distractions to keep us from seeing how he is constantly trying to destroy souls.

A constant distraction is that he keeps Christians fighting against each other to turn their attention away from God. If they are not looking and depending on Father God, they can be swayed toward his side. In the story about Job, for example, he wanted Job (through Job's wife) to give up, curse God and turn his back on God (Job 2:9). Job was a man of integrity. He believed in, trusted, and never blasphemed the LORD's Holy name (Exodus 22:28). When Satan was allowed to afflict Job, he wanted him to think that he, Satan, was omnipotent and more significant than God. He wanted Job to reject God and worship him. How ludicrous because Job knew about the greatness, the power, the majesty, and the glory of God as stated in 1 Chronicles 29:11-13. All power and authority come from God, including Satan's power. Job didn't worry about God letting him down; we Christians shouldn't worry either. The God of all creation put Satan under his feet. He banished him to the earth, which is his footstool, never to bask in the glory of God again (Acts 7:49-50).

Of course, Satan is angry. He knows that he and his demons' time to war against us is short (Revelation 11:12-13). So, Satan controls the demons and uses his power to fight against believers and their children. These demons or rebellious angels are real. They are not fantasies as depicted on Hollywood movie screens. Play around with them, and they will eat you and your offspring alive (Revelation 12:9). You are just a tasty morsel to them unless you have the blood of Jesus in you and covering you. They don't like the blood of Jesus. Through the blood of Jesus, we are saved from our sins (Leviticus 17:11 NKJV). The demons don't want us saved. They want us to remain in sin so death and destruction can take us. As believers, we have power. We can fight back. We can fight against Satan for our children's souls. We have the word of God, the Holy Bible, which trains us to use the weapons of warfare against his wicked kingdom. The horrible things of war will remain until this world ends. After that, God will make a New Heaven and a New Earth. We must wear battle garments, watch, pray, and continue fighting until renewal comes. We should do as Apostle Paul told Timothy (1 Timothy 6:12) fight the good fight.

CHAPTER 5

Stand in the Gap

I n military terms, standing in the breach means holding back an attack from the enemy when other defenses have failed. Some parents or guardians are not good soldiers. They run at the sound of the enemy coming. They are selfish and uncaring. "Can a mother abandon her child?" God asked in Isaiah 49:15 (NASB). The answer is yes. For sundry reasons, women discard their children like rubbish every day. For example, children are found in dumpsters, on doorsteps, and even in shallow graves.

Nevertheless, God will not forget or abandon any children he sends here to this earth. All of us are the LORD God's children, young and old, and he loves each of us so much that he sent his son, Jesus, to take the death penalty for us. Children are so important that God tattooed their names on the palms of his hand (Isaiah 49:16). When a baby cries, a mother goes to see about him. She wants to love and comfort her child. Is God so different? Aren't we God's children who he looks over and takes care of? When a child of this world who has been murdered, aborted, or killed in another way cries out, don't you think Jesus hears them? (Psalms 72:12-14). When the children of Israel cried out to God, he heard them. At a most critical moment of anguish, while hanging on the cross, Jesus cried out, and God heard him (Psalms 22:1-5; Matthew 27:45-46). Jesus knew what it was like to have his life's blood spilled by vengeful, hateful, ignorant people. Yet he forgave them all.

In Ecclesiastes 1:9 (KJV), King Solomon once said, "There is nothing new under the sun." In the Old Testament, people sacrificed their children to the pagan god Molech by throwing them into the fire (2 Kings 23:10; Jeremiah 7:31 NLT). Today, people offer their children to the god of technology and airwaves. Anywhere they can get a satellite signal, they connect. They start introducing children as young as infants to technology. They fatten these children on iPhones, I-pads, laptops, etc., and any other new device that comes out, thus allowing them to be devoured by Satan, the prince of the power of the air (Ephesians 2:2; John 5:19 NIV). Don't get me wrong, the devices are not harmful. Some technological devices have been used to save many lives. However, the non-supervision and misuse of these devices hurt children. When parents or guardians are not watching their children, it leaves access to principalities, powers, dominions, and rulers of darkness to get into these devices, thus destroying children's minds and souls. Because there is no supervision or limits set with these devices, children learn to disconnect from mankind and form a bond with the evil beings attached to these wireless inanimate objects. Children are being taught to worship technology instead of the LORD God of all creation.

Remember, God is jealous (Exodus 20:1-5). Christians are commanded in the Holy Bible to train their children in the ways of the LORD (Proverbs 22; Deuteronomy 6:7). The world is in rebellion against God. They also follow their father, Satan, and teach their children to follow him (John 8: 42-44). They do not wrestle against the powers of darkness because they are already a part of it. They have no love for themselves, their children, or anyone else because love dwells in the light. Therefore, they listen to Satan when he tells them to hate, maim, or disfigure their children's bodies, minds, and lives. Satan leads them to abuse and neglect their children so the evil beings out there can kill, steal, and destroy them.

But hold on; all is not lost. We have a God who sits high and looks low. He is sovereign. His eyes don't miss anything in Heaven or on Earth (Psalms 33:13-14; Hebrews 4:13). He allows things to happen because he is patient and merciful. He has given us time to repent from our evil ways and return to him. The Holy Father waits for judgment day when all evil and rebellion will end (Malachi 4:1). In the meantime, Christians have the authority to stand in the gap (Ezekiel 22:30) while fighting and protecting the souls of their children. One way of standing in the gap is by meditating on the words of God and speaking those words, which will activate the power to fight Satan, the enemy (Hebrews 4:12). Know this!

You will get attacked when you take faith and stand up for your children or anybody's children. Since you are no longer a part of Satan's kingdom, he will attack you or the weakest part of you. That's why we are told in Ephesians 6:10-18 to put on the whole armor of God. When you do this, you are covered by the blood of the Lamb of God. There is power in the blood. It is a spiritual weapon that gives us victory. It is also a part of your battle garments. Your children need you, and you need this divine protection. Following God's rules and plans will protect us from the enemy's fiery darts (Psalms 27:1-2). The Lord said that he would never leave or forsake us (Deuteronomy 31:6). He is our strength and protection (Psalms 46:1). God is our Commander in Chief, and we are on the battlefield all the time.

CHAPTER 6

Judgement Day (The Final Victory)

God's spirit, which dwells inside us, is more significant than any spirit in the world, we hold ultimate power because God is protecting us. He gave us his spirit of power, love, and a sound mind (2 Timothy 1:7). Therefore, we are not fearful of entering any battle (Romans 8:31; Isaiah 41:10; Joshua 1:9). The LORD said in Ezekiel 18:4 that all souls are his. As Christians, we spread the gospel of our LORD Jesus Christ and fight battles so that no soul will be lost. The spiritual war with Satan will end, and God's Day of judgment is coming. The LORD God has the final word. He will judge every action that every fleshly or spiritual being has done in Heaven or on Earth (Revelation 20:11-15; Jude

1:6; 2 Peter 2:4 ESV). In the Holy Bible, God's word already tells us the exact punishment that will be received for disobedience, rebellion, and sin. There will be no surprises because the wages of sin are death, and the gift of God is ternal life through Jesus Christ (Romans 6:23). The Father waits patiently for humankind to repent. He gives us chances repeatedly. No one knows when the time will end except God. According to the Holy Bible, not even his son, Jesus, or any angels know when God will say that's enough (Mark 13:32-33; Revelation 3:3). Brothers and Sisters, we know that Satan has already been defeated in Heaven and on Earth (Revelation 12:10-12). The Holy angels defeated him in Heaven (Revelation 12:7-9). Jesus Christ defeated him on the cross, taking the keys to death and hell from him (Revelation 1:17). The saints of God also defeated him on earth by the Lamb's blood and the word of their testimony (Revelation 12:11). Satan has been allowed free reign over the earth for a short while, but His day and punishment are coming soon (Revelation 20:10; John 12:31). He will be judged, and eternal fire is what he will reap (Matthew 25:41). The good news is that as Christians our sins have already been judged on the cross when we repented and accepted Jesus Christ as our LORD and Savior. The death penalty was lifted from us (John 5:24 ESV). Our works will be judged on that great day of judgment, not our souls (1 Corinthians 3:13).

What works have we done for the children? God sent them here to be developed spiritually and return to his kingdom. The names of the cowardly, fearful, and disobedient people who will not do right by the children will be omitted from the book of life. These individuals will receive their just punishment in the Lake of Fire that burns forever and ever (Revelation 20:15; 21:8). Be encouraged, dear saints of God. Daily the battle is being fought, but the victory has already been won in Jesus' name. When we call on the name of Jesus, victory is ours (Romans 8:34-39). Overwhelming victory comes through following the life and teachings of Jesus Christ, who loves our children and us.

CHAPTER 7

Questions for Reflection and Discussion

I. MAN OUT OF MANKIND:

Q. Why don't these evil spirits just leave me and my children alone?

A. Being no match for God's Holy angels in Heaven and being banished to the earth, Satan is still raging mad and has turned his anger towards us mortal beings. No one escapes his wrath. The Lord Jesus, after pulling off his heavenly garments and coming to this earth as a human baby, was attacked too. Satan used king Herod to try to kill Jesus. All human beings, including you and your children, come under his radar for attack and destruction (Mathew 1:18-25; 6:10; Philippians 2:5-8).

In the book of Genesis, we see that man's power and permission to reproduce came directly from the mouth of God himself. We are the sons and daughters of God. Once saved, we become spiritually bred to look and act more and more like Jesus. On the other hand, angels are servants and not sons of God. They are spirit beings created to serve God and us, his children. They are never to be worshiped. They do not marry or reproduce their kind. According to the Holy Bible, they were never told to be fruitful and multiply. Their whole purpose is to do the express will of God, and God uses them in any way he chooses.

Genesis 1:11-28; John 14:9-11; Hebrews 1:5-7; Matthew 22:23-30.

II. TRANSFORMATION FROM NATURAL TO SPIRITUAL:

Q. Can a natural-minded man walk in the spiritual realm without being transferred to the spirit?

A. The natural-minded or fleshly man has ever received Jesus Christ as his Lord and savior. He has not been regenerated. This kind of man functions entirely on human wisdom. He is an unbeliever and relies on human logic to succeed in life. The natural-minded man cannot understand the things of God and calls it foolishness. He is an enemy of God and a follower of Satan. He can never receive anything from God in his fallen state because he considers himself right in his eyesight. The natural-minded man is spiritually blind and unable to walk in the spiritual realm. Unless his mind is transferred from flesh to spirit, he will never be able to enter the kingdom of God.

1 Corinthians 2:14; Proverbs 21:2-4; John 3:6; James 3:13-17.

Q. If I have been born again, does that mean that I have been transferred to the Spirit?

A. Yes. You do not experience a second physical or natural birth when you are born again; instead, your heart and mind are changed to the spiritual. Your human spirit has been regenerated. You are no longer a sinner full of hatred toward God. You are changed from the inside out and have a new life in Christ. You love God and want to please him by following his word.

John 3:7; Romans 8:7; 2 Corinthians 5:17; Ezequiel 36:26.

III. SPIRITUAL BLINDNESS:

Q. If people can see angels, then why can't they see demons?

A. People have been encountering and interacting with the good and evil angels since man entered the earth. Some examples from the Bible are Adam and Eve, whom Lucifer, the fallen angel, tricked. Some shepherds saw a company of angels that announced Christ's birth. After seeing how a demonic spirit tormented his son, a father brought his child to Jesus to be healed. Satan tempted the LORD Jesus for 40 days and 40 nights. After his ordeal, heavenly angels came to his aid and ministered to his needs. Lastly, Apostle Peter was released from prison by an angel.

Luke 2:8-15; Genesis 3:1-13; Luke 9:37-42; Matthew 4:1-11; Acts 12:6-11; Ephesians 4:18.

Q. A lot of people are spiritually blind. Why do I have to change?

A. Some people don't want to change. The LORD God gives each person in this world free choice. Some choose darkness rather than light. Satan, the god of this world, blinds the eyes of unbelievers. He wants them to worship him only. He does not want anyone to see or even be on the side of righteousness. Because God is light and there is no darkness in him, Satan wants us to stay away from God. He doesn't wish the unbelievers to see the truth that their souls are headed toward destruction. He wants as many souls as possible to follow him and his cohorts into the Lake of Fire that burns forever and ever. Therefore, people who don't want to change will reap what they sow.

Proverbs 4:26-27; Deuteronomy 30:19; Galatians 6:7-8.

IV. SPIRITUAL WARFARE:

Q. Demons or fallen angels possess superhuman powers, what are they afraid of?

A. Angels are afraid of God, the Father, and his son, Jesus Christ. God created them and can eradicate them at any given moment. They fear and tremble at the presence of God. They know that all power is in God's hands in Heaven and Earth. Angels know that disobedience will get them locked in chains of darkness to await judgment. They also know that when God says, "go left," and they go right, their proverbial *goose is cooked* for being disobedient to the word of God. Our Holy Father does not tolerate disobedience. Man cannot get away with it, nor can angels. It took believing in Jesus and his shed blood to get us humans out of hot water with God. Angels don't have an advocate.

2 Peter 2:14; Matthew 8:28-29; Matthew 6:10; Romans 13:1-2; James 2:19.

Q. What are some of the weapons of warfare?

A. Some of the weapons of warfare are love, prayer, faith, belief, fasting, word of testimony, word of God, and the Holy Spirit.

Hebrews 4:12; Revelation 12:11; Ephesians 6:18; Matthew 17:21; Ephesians 3:20; 1 Thessalonians 5:8; John 1:1.

V.   STAND IN THE GAP:

Q. If I do nothing and don't stand in the gap for my child what will happen?

A. According to the Bible, every human being has sinned. We were born in and shaped in it. Sin and rebellion caused a gap between God and us. Sin brings about death and eternal damnation. The best news is that Jesus, our mediator, closed the gap for us. After we are saved, we should share the gospel so that others can come to know the Lord Jesus and have their sins pardoned. We should be making intercessory prayers and supplications with thanksgiving to God for others who are lost. Your children included. Rachel, in the Bible, wept for her children. Have you ever cried out to God for your children? Teaching them to love God and follow the Lord's ways is standing in the gap. Praying over your children and living godly lives before them is standing in the gap. Doing nothing allows ungodly worldly values to shape your child's mind and spirit. Remember, the world loves its kind. Also, your children could become unfit to enter the Kingdom of God if you do nothing.

1 John 2:15-17; Deuteronomy 6:7; Romans 3:23; Matthew 28:16; Ezekiel 18:4; Proverbs 22:6.

Q. How long do I stand in the gap for my child?

A. By standing in the gap, you are interceding for your children. You are lifting their souls to the heavenly Father for reasons deemed of the utmost importance to you. Love helps you stand and fight for your cause. While standing there, the Holy Spirit will remind you of God's promise to you and your family. Whether your child is two or 72 years old, they will always be your offspring. Stand for as long as you need to. God hears a mother's prayer. Hannah, Elizabeth, Mary, and the Canaanite (Syrophoenician) woman are examples of mothers in the Bible who prayed for their children.

John 15:12-13; 2 Chronicles 7:14-26; Romans 8:34; 1 Peter 3:12; Matthew 15:21-30.

VI. JUDGMENT DAY (THE FINAL VICTORY):

Q. Thinking about Judgment Day makes me afraid. How do I learn the truth about it?

A. Judgment day is a day set apart by God in which he will judge the entire human race for disobeying his written word. The whole truth about what will happen on Judgement Day is written in the Holy Bible. Everything has been documented from Genesis to Revelation for your knowledge. Don't forget that Satan and the renegade angels will be judged too. God's judgment will be just and in righteousness. The wicked will be sentenced to everlasting punishment. On the other hand, the Saints will be given the gift of eternal life in the presence of God, our Father, and his son, Jesus Christ. Everyone will receive something from the hand of God.

Hebrews 9:27; Revelation 20:11-15; John 5:28-29; Romans 4:7-8, 21-26; Matthew 25:46; John 3:17-18.

Q. How am I victorious?

A. Not only does the Lord Jesus have the final victory on judgment day, but you do too. The Holy Father gives you the gift of victory for having faith in Jesus. Namely, you have divine triumph over darkness, death, sin, sickness, the world, and Satan. You have the victory now while living in this world, and when you pass from this life into eternity.

John 5:1-4; 1 Corinthians 15:54-58; Deuteronomy 20:4; Colossians 2:13-15.

A PRAYER FOR PARENTS

Most gracious Heavenly Father who is, was, and will be forever more; I come to you in the name of Jesus. I humble myself before your throne, asking for help and blessings on parents, guardians, and others reading this book. I also ask the same thing of anyone with a heart to protect your little children. This very day, I ask that you grant them wisdom, knowledge, peace, and strength to battle the evil forces out there trying to destroy your children. Oh, merciful Father, shower your blessings upon these warriors. Let them feel your mighty power. Please wrap your strong, loving arms around them as a shield of protection while they do spiritual warfare. Give them victories now while they are on this side of glory. When they walk into your everlasting kingdom, let the angels rejoice that they have overcome the enemy. Let them have a hallelujah good time dancing in your presence. Let them bask in the rewards you have set forth for them to receive from the beginning of time. Forgive them for any known or unknown mistakes regarding how they treated your children, Almighty Father Lord of all; help them forgive themselves and others who may have harmed those precious little souls. Open their eyes and lead them on the path you have set forth in your word. Let them not be swayed from righteousness. Dear heavenly Father, I thank you, praise you, and bless your Holy name for hearing my prayer. In the mighty name of Jesus, Amen.

ABOUT THE AUTHOR

Vanessa M. White is an avid writer. She aspires to become one of the greatest storytellers in her field. She is retired Law Enforcement Officer who worked for 24 and a half years in jails and prisons combined. By the election of God, she has been called and chosen to walk in the office of an Evangelist. She has a great love and compassion for children. She wants them to grow healthy, whole, and complete in the knowledge and love of our Lord and Savior, Jesus Christ.

Other books by Vanessa M. White: *Sugar and Honey.*

Printed in the United States
by Baker & Taylor Publisher Services